621

released for sale

DENMEAD MIDDLE
SCHOOL LIBRARY

MACHINES

Mark Lambert
and Alistair Hamilton-MacLaren
Illustrations by Stephen Wheele

Exploring Technology

Communications
Flight
Houses and Homes
Land Transport
Machines
Structures
Textiles
Water Transport

Series Editor: Sue Hadden
Book Editor: Elizabeth Spiers
Designer: Malcolm Walker, Kudos Designs

Cover: Mechanical diggers
in operation on a building site.

First published in 1991 by
Wayland (Publishers) Ltd
61 Western Road, Hove
East Sussex BN3 1JD, England

© Copyright 1991 Wayland (Publishers) Ltd

**British Library Cataloguing in
Publication Data**
Lambert, Mark *1946–*
  Machines.
  1. Machinery
  I. Title II. Hamilton-Maclaren, Alistair
  III. Series
  621.8

  ISBN 0-7502-0039-1

Phototypeset by Nicola Taylor, Wayland
Printed in Italy by G. Canale & C.S.p.A.,
  Turin
Bound in France by A.G.M.

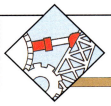

Contents

Machines and people	4
Levers	6
Build a ballista	
Wheels, gears and pulleys	8
Using pulley blocks	
Time machines	10
Build a water clock	
Inclined planes	12
Make a micrometer	
Wind machines	14
Make a windmill	
Control systems	16
Build a traffic-light system	
Steam engines	20
Make a steam turbine	
Internal combustion engines	22
Electrical machines	24
Build an electric motor	
Generators	26
Generating electricity	
Sorting machines	28
Make sorters	
Pumps	30
An Archimedes screw pump	
Machines in the home	32
An automatic curtain-puller	
Computers	34
Make a data sorter	
Automation	36
Build a remote-control gate	
Robots	38
Build a robot arm	
Machines of the future	42
Glossary	44
Further information	46
Index	47

Machines and people

Machines come in all shapes and sizes. Clocks, dishwashers and cars are all described as machines. But what is it that all these things have in common? What makes them different from the things that are not machines?

The answer is simple. Machines do work, and because machines are invented by people, they do work for people. Some machines are used to make people's work easier. For example, a lever (see page 6) can help to lift something off the ground. The lever makes the task easier because the person operating it has to use less effort. Many other machines do all or most of the work for us. An engine, for example, runs by itself without the need for human effort.

What, then, is work and how is it achieved? Scientists say that doing work is using energy to make something move or warm up. Energy is a vital part of this process; without energy no work can be done. There are many forms of energy, including electrical energy, chemical energy, kinetic (moving) energy and heat energy. Different machines use different forms of energy in order to produce work. The energy is converted into a completely different form during the process.

For example, in a car engine, the chemical energy in fuel is converted into heat energy. This is, in turn, converted into kinetic energy. This kinetic energy is used to drive the wheels of the car, and is converted into heat energy in the process. In the end, all of the chemical energy contained in the fuel is lost to the surroundings as heat. But meanwhile, work has been done; the car has been moved along the road.

In an everyday sense, we define work as carrying out a particular task. Thus, a washing machine cleans clothes, a vacuum cleaner picks up dust, a drill bores a hole and a kettle boils water. Opening a door is work, as is building a house. However, in all these cases, work is still carried out in the scientific sense; it is just that several work stages may be performed before the task is completed.

Today, we tend to think of machines as being very complex. It is true that many of them are, but it is important to remember that they have all been developed gradually from much simpler machines. Their origins can be traced back through earlier, simpler machines to the simplest machines of all. There are just two types of these – the lever and the inclined plane, or wedge.

Machines can be used to do a great deal of the hard work when carrying out such tasks as building houses and transporting goods.

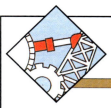

Levers

A lever is a bar or rod pivoted at one point. The pivot point is known as the fulcrum. An effort is applied at some point on the lever in order to move a load situated at another point.

There are three classes of lever. In a first-class lever, the fulcrum is between the effort and the load, like a see-saw. This type of lever gives the user what is called a mechanical advantage; in other words, the user has to use less effort to move the load. This is achieved by placing the effort much further from the fulcrum than the load. The user has to do exactly the same amount of work using the lever, but less effort is needed at any moment. This is because the point at which the effort is applied moves through a much greater distance than the load. Examples of tools that use the first-class lever principle are a crowbar and a pair of pliers.

In a second-class lever, the load is between the fulcrum and the effort. As long as the load is much closer to the fulcrum than the effort, the user can get a mechanical advantage. Again, this is because the effort moves over a greater distance than the load. A pair of nutcrackers is a second-class lever.

In a third-class lever, the effort is between the load and the fulcrum. There is no mechanical advantage as the effort moves a smaller distance than the load, as it is closer to the fulcrum.

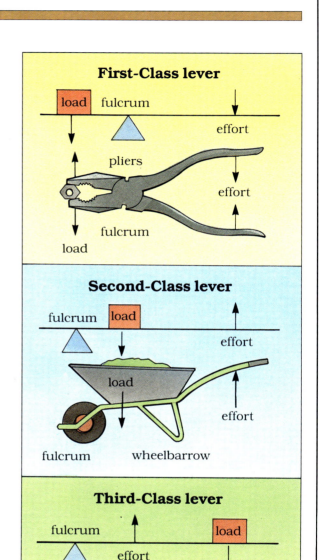

Build a ballista

You need:
Ping-Pong balls
Wood base (150 mm x 75 mm x 20 mm)
Wood pivot arm (200 mm x 20 mm x 12 mm)
2 wood sides (75 mm x 50 mm x 6 mm)   2 nails (25 mm long)
4 screws (25 mm; no. 6)
Drill with 6 mm diameter bit
6 mm diameter dowel (300 mm long)
Old felt-tip pen casing, to fit dowel
Screwdriver   Egg carton
Hammer   Wood glue
Rubber band   Ruler
6 fencing staples   Hacksaw
2 cotton reels

1. Shape the two sides to your own design. In each side, drill one 6 mm hole for the pivot. Drill two more holes for the fixing screws, as shown.

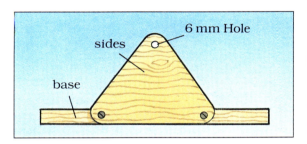

2. Fix a nail in one end of the base, leaving about 5 mm sticking out. Fix four staples to the bottom of the base, not too tightly. Glue and screw the sides to the base. Cut two 100 mm lengths of dowel for the axles. Cut each cotton reel in half, for the wheels. Slide in the axles and glue the wheels to them.

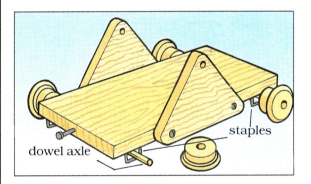

3. Fix a nail to one end of the pivot arm. Fix two staples to the underside of the pivot arm, not too tightly. Cut out a ball cup from the egg carton. Glue the ball cup to the pivot arm. Cut two spacers, about 25 mm long, from the felt-tip pen casing. Slide the dowel through one spacer, the two staples and the other spacer. Glue and fit the dowel in position. Fix the rubber band to the two nails.

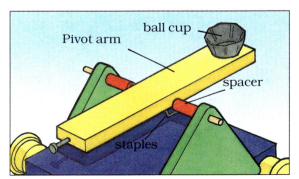

4. Paint your ballista. Test it, firing the Ping-Pong balls at arms' length.

Wheels, gears and pulleys

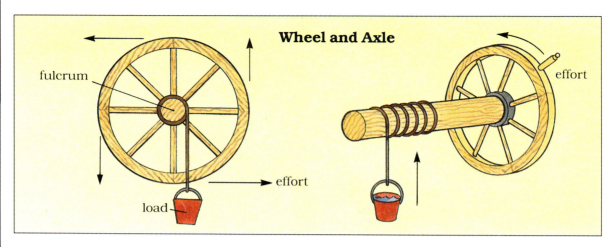

A wheel with an axle may not look much like a lever, but in fact that is just what it is. Think of the centre of the wheel as the fulcrum and imagine a single spoke (the lever) running from the centre to the outer rim. Effort is applied at the end of the spoke, the wheel turns and a load on the axle is moved.

A simple example of a wheel and axle is a winch, as used to draw water from a well. However, the most familiar form of wheel and axle is the type used in a wheeled vehicle, such as a cart. In this case, the load is the friction force generated between the axle and its support.

A pulley is another kind of wheel, with a groove set in the outer rim, so that a rope, belt or chain can be attached. If a rope, belt or chain is combined with two or more pulleys (see project opposite), mechanical advantage can be gained. As with a simple lever, the effort moves through a greater distance than the load.

Gears are wheels with teeth, or cogs, around the rim. They are used to transfer movement from one moving part of a machine to another (for example, from bicycle pedals to the wheels). The greater the difference between the two gear wheels, the greater the mechanical advantage.

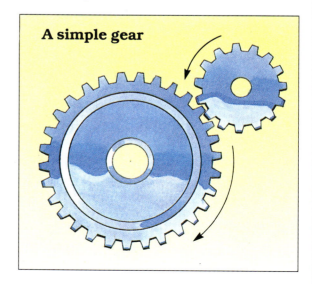

Using pulley blocks

You need:
2 plastic pulleys (20-40 mm diameter, with 4 mm diameter holes)
3 m strong cord
Wood (400 mm x 50 mm x 6 mm)
6 x 4 mm diameter nuts with bolts 40 mm long
Felt-tip pen casing (must be at least 4 mm diameter)
2 small buckets of sand and trowel
Hacksaw   Ruler
Drill with 4 mm bit
Strong beam, firmly secured

1. Cut out four sides from the wood, for the pulley blocks. Each should be 100 mm long. Mark lines 20 mm in from each end. In the centre of each line, drill 4 mm diameter holes. Drill another hole exactly in the centre of each side. Cut four spacers from the pen casing, each 3 mm longer than the thickness of the pulleys. Fit the sides, pulleys, spacers, nuts and bolts together as shown. Do not overtighten the central nut.

2. Tie one pulley block securely to the strong beam. Thread the cord through the block. Put some sand into one of the buckets and tie it to one end of the cord. Tie the other bucket to the cord, so that it is hanging off the ground. Shovel in sand until both buckets just balance. Untie the buckets.

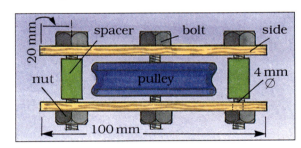

3. Thread the pulley system as shown. Tie one bucket (the load) on to the bottom pulley block. Tie the second bucket (the effort) to the rope. See how much sand must be removed to balance the buckets again.

4. Try building more pulleys into your system and measure the effect on the effort bucket.

Time machines

Early clocks were simple devices. The passing of time was measured by the rate at which a candle burned, or the rate at which sand or water flowed out of a container. Anything that happens at a regular rate can be used to mark the passing of time.

Traditional clocks are machines that use levers, wheels and gears. For example, a pendulum clock has a lever called a pendulum. If it is allowed to swing freely, a pendulum always swings at the same rate, no matter how far it swings from side to side. A pendulum has its fulcrum at the upper end. It is kept in motion by being given a tiny push at the end of each swing. This is achieved by a toothed wheel, known as the escape wheel, and a device known as the escapement, which is attached to the pendulum.

The escape wheel is driven by a spring, or by a weight on the end of a cable wound round an axle. The driving power is transmitted to the escape wheel by a chain of gears.

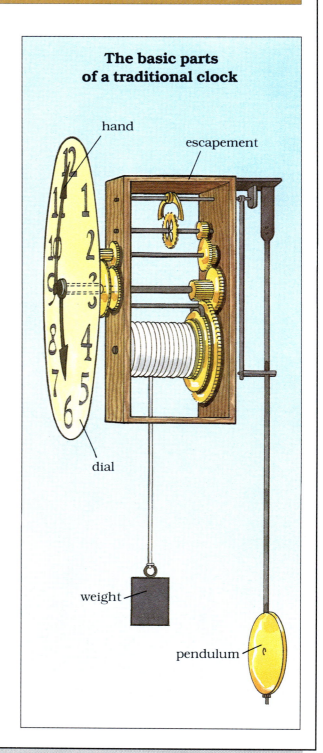

A diagram to show the basic features of a traditional, or mechanical, clock. This type of clock was probably developed in the monasteries during the Middle Ages. This particular clock is controlled by a pendulum, which swings at a constant rate.

Build a water clock

You need:
3 litre plastic drink bottle
40 mm diameter waste pipe (175 mm long)
Piece of polystyrene packing
Hacksaw
Large plastic container
Stiff brass wire
Wood (1 m x 50 mm x 25 mm)
Selection of nails and screws
Hammer
Screwdriver
Marker pen
File
Plastic glue
Watch with second hand

1. Build a simple frame from the wood, to support the clock parts. Carve a small float from the polystyrene. It should slide easily up and down the waste pipe.

2. Cut the bottom off the drink bottle to make the holding tank. Stick the waste pipe (guide tube) on the inside, just up from the base. Mount the drink bottle on the frame with the waste pipe vertical.

3. Cut the lever and scale from the plastic container. Fix the lever to the frame, so that the float end is centrally over the guide tube. Make a coupling rod from stiff brass wire and fix it to the float. Fix the other end of the coupling rod to the lever, so that the pointer is at its highest position when there is no water in the holding tank.

4. Set the frame up near a tap, so that water drips into the holding tank. Adjust the flow so that the tank is almost full in one hour. Empty the tank and mark the zero (no water) point on the scale. Use your watch to help you mark the other positions on the scale as time passes.

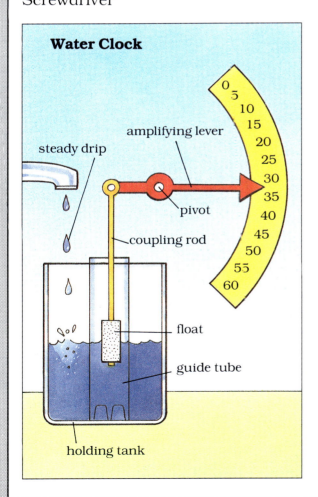

11

Inclined planes

An inclined plane is a sloping surface. At first glance, it might seem to have a limited range of uses, but in fact, the inclined plane is the basis of many modern tools and machines.

A wedge is a type of inclined plane. It is useful because it can be pushed between two surfaces. A wooden wedge makes an excellent door stop and a metal one (such as an axe head) can be used to split logs. A nail and a chisel are also wedges. A saw is just a blade edged with many tiny chisels and the surface of a file is covered with even smaller wedges.

A spiral inclined plane is even more useful. We usually call this a

A selection of tools that work by using one or more inclined planes.

screw thread, a device that we would find it hard to do without. Screws, bolts and other similar kinds of fastening all use the principle of the screw thread. A screw jack is a commonly used device for raising heavy objects (such as a car) off the ground. The first known screw device was invented over 2,000 years ago by the Greek scientist Archimedes. His machine used a screw thread inside a tube to raise water from a river into nearby fields, and similar devices are still used in some places today.

Make a micrometer

1. Cut about 50 mm from the base of the bottle. Make a hole exactly in the centre of the base, so that the threaded rod is a tight fit. Fix the rod securely at one end, with a nut on either side.

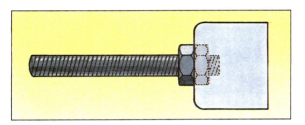

You need:
100 mm length of metal threaded rod, with 3 nuts to fit (M16 ideal)
Washing-up liquid bottle
Base board (150 mm x 75 mm x 12 mm)
Board for end pieces (50 mm x 75 mm x 12 mm)
Stiff wire (100 mm)
Epoxy resin
Screws with nuts to fit
Screwdriver
Steel rule with mm divisions
Hacksaw   Glue

2. Cut out two end pieces as shown. Glue and screw these pieces to the base board. Glue a nut to one of the supports, as shown, and leave to dry.

3. Screw the rod through the nut, until it touches the support on the other side. Do not force it. Screw the indicator wire on to the base, and bend it to line up with the middle of the drum (washing-up liquid bottle base).

4. To set the scale, mark a line on the indicator drum level with the indicator wire pointer. Unscrew the rod ten turns of the drum and measure the distance between the end of the rod and the support, as shown. Divide this distance by 10. This equals the length of one turn of the drum. Divide the drum evenly into ten parts. Your micrometer now measures to 1/10 of a turn.

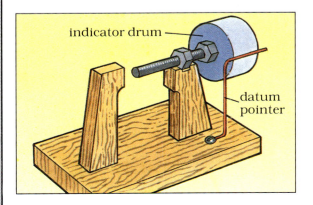

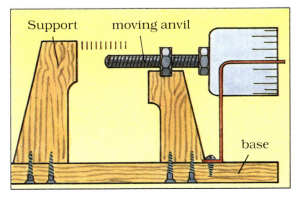

Wind machines

So far, we have looked at very simple machines. More complicated machines are usually combinations of levers and inclined planes. A windmill is a good example of this type of machine.

Windmills have been used for over 1,000 years for pumping water and grinding corn into flour. A typical windmill has flat sails set at an angle to the wind. They are inclined planes. Wind striking the front of the sail assembly causes each sail to move sideways, making the whole assembly rotate. In a modern windmill, used for generating electricity, the sails are shaped like the wings of an aeroplane for greater

A traditional Dutch windmill with four inclined planes that form the sails.

efficiency. Some modern windmills have sails with horizontal blades, but these, too, are inclined planes.

Inside the tower of a windmill, there are many levers. Most of these are wheels and axles, and a number of the wheels are gears. They are used to convert the movement of the sails into movement for driving the grinding wheels or pump. In fact, a windmill can be thought of as a huge wheel and axle (the sail assembly and its shaft) used to drive a grinding wheel or pump.

Make a windmill

You need:
Ground stake (75 mm x 75 mm x 2 m)
Small-diameter steel tube
Ball bearing to fit tube
Nut and bolt (50 mm long, to fit freely in tube)
Pine base (300 mm x 50 mm x 25 mm)
2 pieces exterior ply (300 mm x 200 mm x 6 mm and 600 mm x 150 mm x 6 mm)
Dowel (9 mm diameter) 4 x 225 mm
Dowel (6 mm diameter) 1 x 150 mm
Wood cube (about 50 mm sides)
Polythene carrier bag
Sticky plastic tape
Selection of nails and screws
Drill with 2 mm, 6 mm and 9 mm bits
2 cotton reels
2 cable ties
Compass
Thin cord
Hammer
Screwdriver
Hacksaw
Scissors

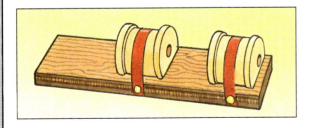

1. Build the pivot tube and base as described in Project 9. Saw off a small lengthwise section of each cotton reel. Glue them on to the base. Hold them firmly in place with the cable ties.

2. Drill the wood cube with one 6 mm and two 9 mm holes. Glue and push the 6 mm dowel into the cube. This is the rotor spindle. Drill a small hole at one end of each 9 mm dowel for the cord to pass through. Glue and push the dowels into the cube. Thread the cord through the holes and tie it securely.

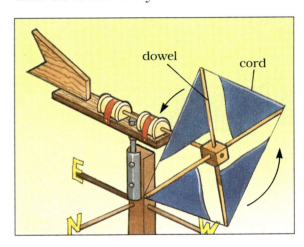

3. Cut a square of polythene of sides 150 mm. Draw the diagonals and cut out the four triangles. Fix these to the dowels and cord using the sticky tape. Make sure that the sheet is wrapped around the dowels.

4. Set up the pivot tube and base outside, well away from buildings and trees. Thread the rotor spindle through the cotton reels. Cut direction indicators from the other piece of ply and fix them below the level of the sails, checking the direction with a compass.

Control systems

Fairground lighting is controlled by rotary switching devices.

Machines can be controlled in various ways. The simplest form of control is a device that turns a machine or system on and off, such as a switch in an electrical circuit. Several switches used together can control a series of connections that control a sequence of events. The project shown overleaf is an example of a rotary switching system. A similar switching system is used to control fairground lighting and message boards in which bulbs light up one after another. Some kinds of programmed washing machine have a rotary device that switches from one part of the washing cycle to the next.

Various mechanical devices are also used to control machines. A cam, for example, can be used to control the position of a lever or wheel. A cam is an offset, or eccentric, shape set on a shaft. Rotating the shaft causes any rod or wheel resting against the cam to change position.

Another commonly used type of control mechanism is known as a hydraulic link. A simple hydraulic link consists of a liquid-filled pipe

A hydraulic ram is operated by pressure in a liquid. When liquid is pumped into the cylinder of the ram, the piston inside the cylinder moves.

with a piston and cylinder at each end. Pressure applied to one piston is transmitted along the pipe and causes the second piston to move. The brakes of a car are operated in this way. The brake pedal is linked to a piston at one end of the system, and there are pistons attached to the brake pads of each wheel. Pressure on the brake pedal is transmitted to the brake pads through the brake fluid in the pipes. Tractors and digging machines also use hydraulic systems to operate lifting arms. The pressure is created by an engine-driven pump and the power is delivered to a jointed arm by a piston-and-cylinder combination known as a hydraulic ram.

Pneumatic links operate in a similar way, but in this case it is air, rather than liquid, that transmits the pressure. The brakes of trains and large lorries are controlled by pneumatic systems.

Other systems can control the speed at which machines operate. A device known as a variable resistor can be used to vary the amount of electricity flowing to a machine. The dimmer switches used in people's homes use a device called a thyristor to achieve the same effect. The speed of an internal combustion engine (see page 22) is controlled by a throttle that varies the amount of fuel fed into the engine.

Build a traffic-light system

You need:
3 x 2.5V light bulbs with holders
On-off switch
2 small silicon diodes (IN4001)
Battery holder with 2 x 1.5V batteries to fit
2 connector blocks
Small screw and washer
4 drawing pins
Paper clip
Pinboard base (100 mm x 100 mm x 12 mm)
Thin strand wire (4 colours), each about 1 m long
Wire strippers
Stiff card
Glue
Scissors
Sticky tape
Cellophane
Drill and bits

1. Drill the base as shown. Attach the switch to the base. Strip the ends of two pieces of wire and connect one side of the switch to the battery and the other side to the screw.

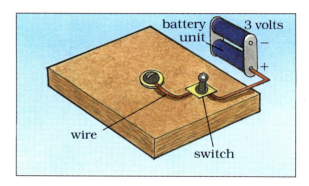

2. Bend one end of the paper clip. Fix down the straight end with the screw and washer. Use the inner loop of the paper clip to draw a circle, as shown. Mark the circle at four equal points.

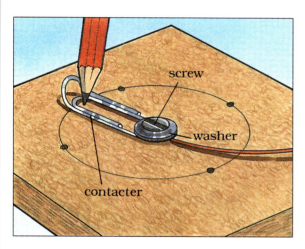

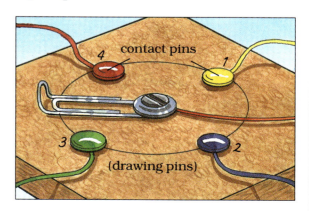

3. Strip the insulation from the ends of four pieces of different-coloured wire. Connect one wire to each drawing pin, and push one into the board at each point. Label the pins.

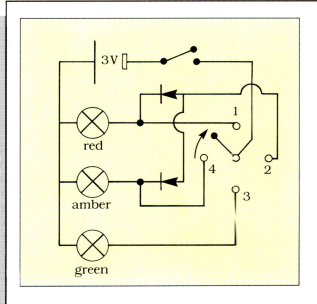

4. Fit the diodes with the band end towards the lights. Use the diagram to help you connect the wires and diodes to the connector blocks.

5. Connect the wires from the switching unit to the bulbs in their holders. Connect the green light to the other side of the battery. Mark each bulb with its colour.

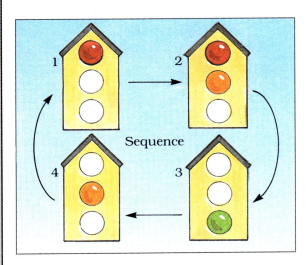

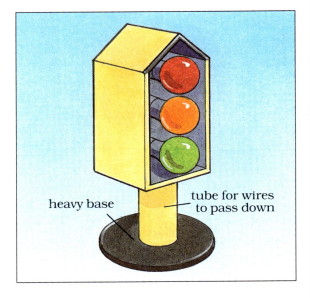

6. Move the paper-clip contactor to pin 1. Turn on the power. The red light should come on. Rotate the contactor steadily, passing over amber, stopping for a while on green, then through amber to red. Wait before repeating.

7. Once you are satisfied that your assembly works, build a lamp housing for your traffic lights, as shown. The windows can be covered in coloured cellophane.

19

Steam engines

Machines do work, and work needs energy. If you do work, such as lifting an object off a table, you use the chemical energy (from food) stored in your body. As your muscles operate, they convert the chemical energy into heat energy, some of which escapes to the air that surrounds you.

A steam engine also converts chemical energy into heat. The chemical energy is contained in the fuel, such as wood or coal, which is burned to produce heat energy. The heat energy is transferred to a boiler containing water, which becomes so energetic that it turns to steam. Steam takes up more space than liquid water, so, if the boiler is enclosed, the pressure of the steam increases.

In a steam engine, steam from the boiler is passed to cylinders. Pistons inside the cylinders move to and fro and the wheels turn.

The energy in the steam is then converted into kinetic (moving) energy in a mechanical device. In some types of steam engine, the steam is fed through one-way valves to a cylinder. Inside the cylinder the steam forces a piston to move to and fro. The piston is linked to a system of levers and wheels that can be used to drive a machine.

In some other steam engines, the steam can be passed to a turbine – a wheel with blades similar to those of a windmill. The pressure of the steam forces the turbine to turn.

Make a steam turbine

You need:
Can with recloseable lid
Disc cut from similar can, with can opener (no more than 120 mm diameter)
Thin metal strip (180 mm x 20 mm)
3 mm diameter metal rod, about 50 mm long
Felt-tip pen casing
Drill with 3 mm bit
Soldering equipment
Heat source
Pliers
Hacksaw

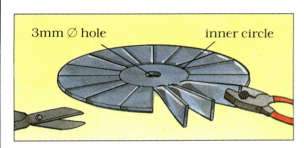

1. Turbine disc: find the centre and drill a 3 mm hole. Divide the circle evenly and snip to the inner circle, as shown. Grip the divisions with the pliers and twist through 90°, all in the same direction.

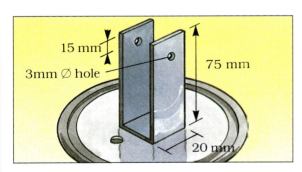

2. Support frame: drill 3 mm holes in the thin metal strip. Bend it to the required lengths and shape. Punch a small hole in the lid of the can. Solder the support to the lid.

3. Make the spacers from the felt-tip pen casing. Make sure they are long enough to centralize the turbine, while allowing it to rotate freely. Bend one end of the spindle (3 mm diameter rod). Thread the other end through the support, spacer, disc, spacer and the other side of the support.

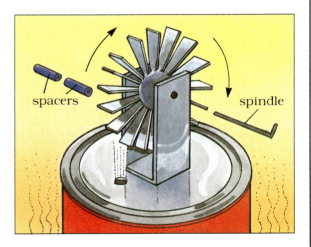

4. Put about 25 mm depth of water in the can and replace the lid. Place the container over the heat, making sure that it cannot tip over. Watch what happens as the water boils. Reduce the heat when the turbine is spinning fast. The lid is a safety valve, so keep well away when the turbine is in operation. Allow the can to cool before attempting to touch it.

Internal combustion engines

A steam engine is called an external combustion engine, because the fuel is burned outside the engine. In an internal combustion engine, the fuel is burned inside the cylinder. As before, the burning fuel generates heat, but this time it is the burning fuel gases that are contained under pressure and used to force the piston down the cylinder.

The most commonly used type of internal combustion engine operates on a four-stroke cycle: that is, the piston moves four times from drawing in fuel to expelling the waste exhaust gases. The first stroke is the induction, or fuel intake, stroke. The inlet valve opens and the piston moves down the cylinder, drawing in a mixture of air and fuel vapour (gas). Then the inlet valve closes and the piston moves up the cylinder, compressing the fuel mixture into a very small space. This is the compression stroke.

The compressed fuel is then ignited by a spark. The burning fuel expands, and as it does so, it forces the piston down again. This is the power stroke. The final stroke is the exhaust stroke – the exhaust valve opens and the piston rises again, pushing the exhaust gases out. The exhaust valve then closes, the inlet valve opens and the cycle begins again.

In a petrol engine, the fuel is ignited by a spark. This is generated across a small gap between two pieces of metal in a spark plug. In a diesel engine, no spark plug is needed. The fuel is not drawn in with the air during the induction stroke. Instead, it is injected into the hot

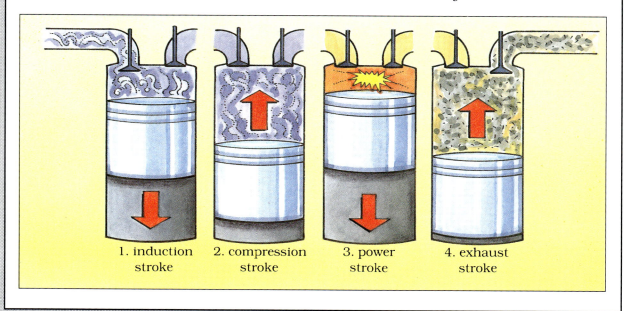

1. induction stroke
2. compression stroke
3. power stroke
4. exhaust stroke

This complex internal combustion engine is used in Ferrari racing cars.

compressed air at the end of the compression stroke. As it mixes with the hot air, it automatically ignites and the power stroke begins.

The up-and-down movement of the piston is of little use, so it has to be converted into a rotating movement. This is achieved by the crankshaft. A simple crankshaft is a shaft with an offset section, known as the crank. This operates on exactly the same principle as a wheel and axle. The lower end of the piston is attached to a piston rod, which in turn is linked to the crank. As the piston moves down on the power stroke, the piston rod pushes the crank downwards and the lever action causes the crankshaft to turn.

In many engines there are two or more cylinders. Each one has a piston linked to a separate crank on the crankshaft. The cylinders fire at different times and this helps to keep the crankshaft turning smoothly.

Electrical machines

Electricity and magnetism are closely related. An electric current generates a magnetic field, and magnetism can be used to generate an electric current. This relationship forms the basis of an electric motor.

A bar magnet has two magnetic poles: a north pole and a south pole. If two magnets are placed close to each other, the north pole of one is attracted to the south pole of the other. On the other hand, two north poles or two south poles repel one another.

A coil of wire carrying an electric current behaves exactly like a bar magnet, with a north pole at one end and a south pole at the other. If such a coil is placed between two other magnets (field magnets) arranged so that two different poles lie near the coil, the north and south poles of the field magnets repel the north and south poles of the coil, which therefore turns.

When the coil, or armature, has turned through 90°, unlike poles start to attract one another. But after another 90° of turn, the electrical connections supplying current to the coil are reversed. The magnetic poles of the coil are also reversed, so it continues to turn. The process continues until the electric current is switched off.

An electric motor converts electricity into kinetic energy.

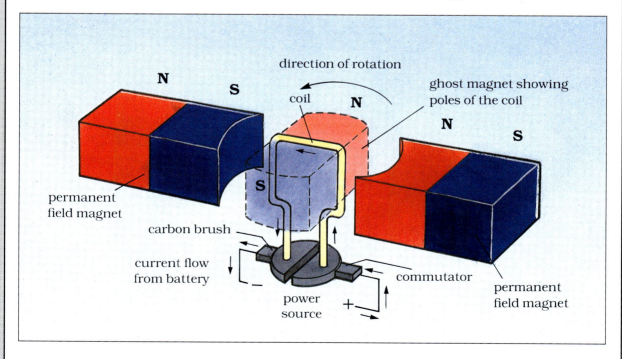

Build an electric motor

You need:
4 x 75 mm nails
2 x 25 mm nails
2 x 25 mm screws
2 felt-tip pen caps
Wood base (150 mm x 75 mm x 20 mm)
Roll of insulated bell wire
Brass foil (40 mm x 15 mm)
Battery
Drill and bits
Hammer
Screwdriver
Sticky tape
Plastic glue
Hacksaw

1. Drill the base with holes for the main nails, as shown. Drive the centre nail right through the base. Wind the wire around the two 75 mm nails, as shown (100 turns on each screw). Tape the coils to prevent unwinding. Drive in the two short nails and screws, as shown. Strip the insulation from the ends of the coil wires and wind them around the screws and the short nails. The bare wire ends should reach to the centre nail. They are the brushes.

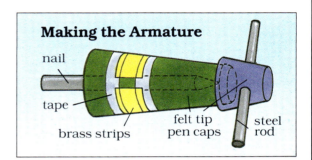

Making the Armature

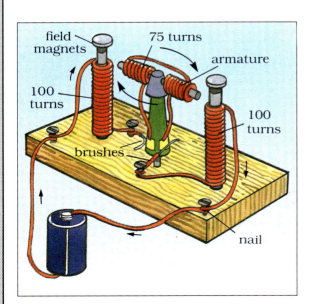

2. Glue and push the two pen tops together. Cut the head and point from a 75 mm nail. Make a tight-fitting hole in the top cap, so that the nail (armature) can be glued in. Put the pen-top assembly on top of the centre nail. Line up the armature with the tops of the field coils, as shown. Take the pen top off again. Hold wire at the base of the pen top and wind the armature, as shown.

3. Cut two foil pieces and fix to the wires. Tape them in position on the pen top, leaving a small gap on each side. Lower the armature on to the centre nail. Adjust the brushes to touch the strips. Connect to the battery and give the armature a small push to start it off.

Generators

Electric motors and generators are devices for converting one form of energy into another. A motor converts electrical energy into kinetic (moving) energy, and a generator does exactly the opposite. The kinetic energy needed to drive a generator may come from any of a range of different sources, such as steam produced by the heat from burning coal, wind, running water or an internal combustion engine.

An electrical generator works on the principle that an electric current is generated in a wire if it is moving through a magnetic field. Thus, if a loop of wire is mechanically rotated between two unlike magnetic poles, an electric current flows through the loop. As long as the loop continues to turn, the current will continue to flow.

The construction of a generator is basically the same as a motor, and in many cases a motor can be used as a generator. In a working electrical generator, the loop is replaced by a coil with many turns. The more turns of wire in the coil, the larger the electric current that is generated.

In a power station, huge generators produce the electricity we use.

Generating electricity

You need:
Ground stake (75 mm x 75 mm x 2 m long)
Small-diameter steel tube
Ball bearing to fit tube
Nut and bolt (50 mm long) to fit in tube
Pine base (300 mm x 50 mm x 25 mm)
Exterior ply (300 mm x 200 mm x 6 mm) for direction vane
Waterproof glue
Selection of nails and screws
Hammer
Screwdriver
Drill and bits
Soldering equipment
Small electric motor and clamp
Propeller
Wire
Fine-reading voltmeter

1. Fix the stake into the ground, well away from buildings and trees. Drill holes in the tube and screw it vertically on to the stake, as shown. Drop the ball bearing into the tube.

2. Drill the pine base 100 mm from one end, to allow the bolt to pass through. Fix the motor clamp at one end and the direction vane at the other end.

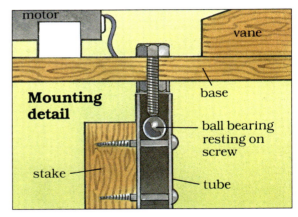

Mounting detail

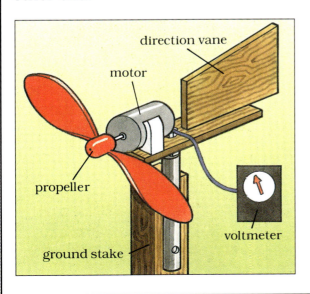

3. Fix the pivot bolt through the hole in the base. Make sure that the propeller is a tight fit on the motor. Solder a long length of wire to the motor terminals. Mount the motor in its clamp and set the pivot bolt into the stake tube. The whole assembly should turn freely. Present the propeller to the wind. Connect a sensitive voltmeter from the motor terminals to the wires. Cut a paper scale for the voltmeter. Mark the highest that the voltmeter reaches in different winds.

Sorting machines

Machines are used to sort letters according to the codes marked on them.

Sorting out two or more different types of item is a task that we often have to do. But sorting large numbers of such items is a very monotonous task, so people have devised machines for the purpose.

A sorting machine has to have two main features. First, there must be some way of distinguishing one type of item from another. Second, there must be a way of separating the items.

In the simplest type of sorting machine, these two processes happen at the same time. In a potato sorter, for example, potatoes are sorted according to size. The potatoes are fed along a conveyor belt and passed over holes of a particular size. Those that are smaller than the holes fall through into a container. Those that are larger pass along into another container.

Other, more complicated, machines are used to sort out such things as coins and letters, using a variety of mechanical and electrical means. Coins may be sorted according to their size or their weight. Letters marked with special dots that show the postal code of the receiver are sorted by electronic machines. Scientists and engineers are beginning to devise machines that recognize and remove reject items emerging from a factory production line.

Make sorters

You need:
A wide range of strips and flat sections
Different lengths of baseboard
Selection of tubes
Selection of rods
Selection of nuts, bolts, screws and nails
Various coins
Hammer
Screwdriver
Hacksaw

Sorting is recognizing differences and grouping into kinds. Differences include size, weight, colour, defect, or type of material. To build a sorting machine, you have to decide what you are going to sort: for example, cubes, balls, coins, rubbish. Then you have to identify the differences within the group. When you know them, you must work out the sequence needed to separate the types (normally the largest or the heaviest first).

When conveyor belts are not available, ramps can be used. They use gravity to move objects through the sorting machine.

Can you use this information to solve the following challenge?
At the end of the day, a car-park attendant must sort the coins from the ticket machine before going home. The machine holds 50p, 20p and 10p coins. Piles of each can then be counted into bags.
Can you design a simple, cheap sorting machine to separate these coins, allowing the attendant to go home earlier?

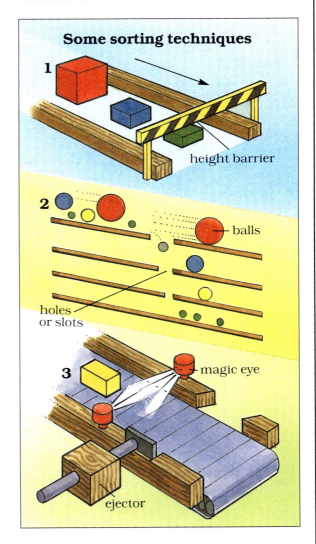

Can you design other sorters: for example, for toy bricks or ball bearings?

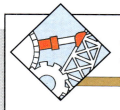

Pumps

A pump is a machine used for moving a liquid from one place to another. Over the centuries, a number of different types of pump have been invented.

The earliest and simplest type of pump is known as a suction or lifting pump. Here, a liquid is drawn up into a cylinder by a piston, allowed to flow past the piston through a one-way valve, and finally lifted out through a nozzle as the piston rises again. The pump may be operated by a handle that works on the lever principle.

This type of pump can only lift water about 7 m because it depends on atmospheric pressure to push the water upwards as the piston is raised. However, a more advanced kind of piston pump, known as a force pump, can raise water over much greater distances. Another variety of piston pump is the diaphragm pump, which has a flexible diaphragm instead of a piston.

A centrifugal pump operates in a completely different way. It has a wheel fitted with vanes. Liquid is drawn towards the centre of the pump and hurled outwards by the vanes as the wheel turns. The liquid that is expelled from the outlet pipe is under greater pressure than the liquid being drawn in.

There are many different types of pump. This kind is known as a lifting pump, as it 'lifts' the water.

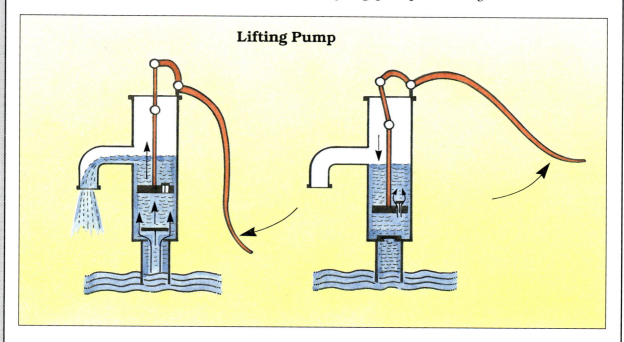

Lifting Pump

An Archimedes screw pump

You need:
Stiff plastic pipe (e.g. gutter fall pipe) about 75 mm diameter x 1 m long
Plastic guttering
3 m garden hose
Strong plastic tape
Waterproof glue
Wood (wide enough to fit in plastic tube)
Metal rod
Large water container
Old stiff plastic bucket
Hacksaw
Drill with bit to fit diameter of metal rod

1. Cut two bungs from the wood, to fit in the 75 mm diameter tube. Drill the centres of the bungs, so that the spindle (metal rod) will fit tightly through. Wind the hose around the tube, to form an even spiral. Fix it securely with plastic tape. Cut supports for the spindle from the plastic bucket, as shown. Drill holes for the spindle to go through. Bend the end of the spindle to make a crank handle and thread it through the supports and the bungs in the tubes. Stick the spindle to the bungs with waterproof glue.

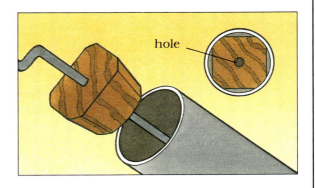

2. Make a delivery chute from the plastic guttering. It can run to another container, or to a sink. Mount the whole assembly over the large water container, as shown. Turn the crank handle steadily.

Could you link this pump to a renewable energy source?

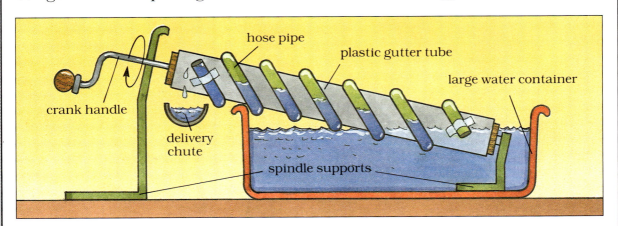

# Machines in the home

A modern kitchen, equipped with labour-saving machines.

A modern home contains a variety of different machines. Many of them have complicated working parts, but they have all developed gradually from much earlier, simpler machines. During the last 100 years or so, technologies based on levers, wheels and inclined planes have been combined with newer technologies based on the movement of electric currents. Electrical machines work by using such currents to create movement or heat. Electronic machines work by controlling very small electric currents in order to store and process information or control the output of other machines.

The machines in your home combine both these types of technology. The food processor or coffee grinder in the kitchen, for example, uses an electric motor combined with chopping blades (inclined planes). The household vacuum cleaner combines an electric motor with an air pump. With the help of other reference books you may be able to work out some of the principles involved in other machines found in people's homes, such as toasters, refrigerators, dishwashers and power tools. Even television and hi-fi sets can be traced back to much simpler devices.

An automatic curtain-puller

You need:
Electric motor with reduction gearbox
Curtain tracks with fittings
Bobbin for winding drum
Nuts and bolts to fit pulley
Power pack for motor
Reversing switch
3 pulleys
Strong cord
Screws
Screwdriver
Drill with bits
Wire
Wirecutters
Base block
2 curtains

1. Fix the curtain track securely to the wall and hang the curtains, making sure that they are fixed at the far ends. Fix two of the pulleys with a nut and bolt to the curtain track, as shown. Fix the third pulley at the other end of the track. Attach the winding drum to the motor and gearbox assembly. Wind several turns of the cord around the drum. Loop the cord over one of the pulleys, round the single pulley, then back over the other pulley in the pair. Wind the end round the drum in the opposite direction to the original winding.

2. To make the control unit, select a very high ratio on the power pack and screw it to the base. Connect it with wires to the motor and gearbox. Attach the reversing switch to the base and connect with wires to the power pack.

3. Centralize the cord by working the winding gear several times in both directions. Close the curtains to overlap, and fix the curtain towing trolleys, one to each cord.

4. Switching the control unit will open or close the curtains. Lubricate the runners for smooth operation.

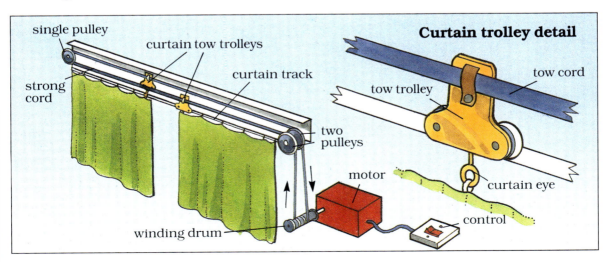

Computers

Modern computers are electronic calculating machines, used for processing and storing information. They are different from the other types of machine we have looked at in this book, as they do not contain moving parts. Instead, they work by controlling the flow of tiny electric currents. However, some of the very early calculating machines were based on complicated arrangements of rods, levers, wheels and gears. It is still possible to use a mechanical device to show how a computer processes information, as in the project shown opposite.

Computers make calculations and process information by using an 'on-off' logic, which means that either something is true or it is not: either a switch is on or it is off. In the cards shown opposite, either there is a hole or there is not. We can represent this logic by a binary, or two-digit code, in which 'on' is represented by 1 and 'off' is represented by 0. An ordinary number can be translated into binary code by using a string of 1s and 0s: for example, 2 in binary code is 10 (one lot of 2 and no lots of 1), 3 is 11 (one-one) and 4 is 100 (one-nought-nought). Thus, a computer can be made to process any information that can be converted into number form.

A Cray II supercomputer can make a billion calculations each second.

Make a data sorter

1. Prepare a data survey for your class, for example: boy/girl, brown/blond hair, blue/brown eyes, tall/short, etc. Each question should have 'yes' or 'no' answers. Make a table to record your survey, recording a 0 for 'yes' and a 1 for 'no'. Later, we will use a hole for 0 and a slot (cut from a hole) for 1.

You need:
At least 20 cards (150 mm x 175 mm – postcards are ideal)
Box to fit cards snugly – you can make this yourself
Paper hole punch with adjustable guide
Knitting needle that slips easily into paper punch holes
Scissors

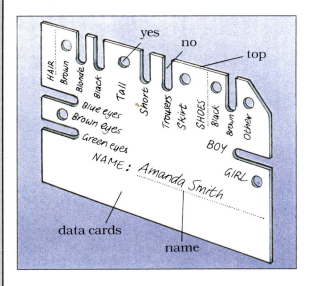

data cards / name

2. Now put the data on to cards. Holes must be in the same place on each card. The more holes, the more information can be recorded. Decide on a sequence for the questions, and punch in one hole for each question. Write in the titles and names, as shown. Compare each card with your survey sheet. Leave a hole for 'yes' and cut a slot for 'no', as shown. Put the cards in the box. Make sure all the holes clear the front of the box.

3. Decide on the first question; e.g. boy/girl. Slide the knitting needle through the appropriate hole. Lift the needle gently, shaking it gently as you raise the cards. If you have chosen girls, all the 'boy' cards should be left in the box. Take them out, and replace them with the ones you have selected.

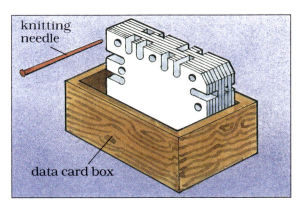

4. Carry on using the cards in the same way, working through all your questions. Eventually, you will have retrieved the data that you want: e.g. girls with brown hair, blue eyes, tall, etc.

Automation

Automatic doors at the entrance to a train station.

It is often convenient to be able to leave a machine to work by itself, without the need for human control or supervision. If the machine's output remains roughly the same all the time, simple control mechanisms can be used (see page 16). But if the machine has several different functions, some sort of automatic control mechanism is necessary.

Automatic control often requires a process known as feedback. In this, the output of the machine is fed into a sensor (detector), whose signals are then used to control the machine itself. For example, a thermostat in a hot-water tank is a temperature-sensitive switch. It switches off the electric current when the water is hot enough, and switches the current on again when the water cools down.

An automatic door also uses a sensor. An infra-red (heat) detector, or a pressure detector in the floor, detects when a person is approaching. The electric signal from the sensor operates a switch, which allows an electric current to operate the door-opening mechanism. If, after a short period of time, the sensor detects nothing, another switch closes and the door is closed again.

Build a remote-control gate

You need:
Wood base (250 mm x 125 mm x 12 mm thick)
Wood pillar (50 mm x 25 mm x 100 mm long)
Wood end support (50 mm x 25 mm x 75 mm long)
Wood anchor (25 mm x 25 mm x 12 mm thick)
Wood pivot plate (75 mm x 20 mm x 12 mm thick)
2 conduit clamps
Barrier (20 mm diameter plastic tube, 200 mm long)
Alloy strip (12 mm x 2 mm x 175 mm)
2 ml syringe and cable grip to fit barrel
500 mm plastic tube to fit syringes
Selection of screws, nuts and bolts
1 m stiff wire   Screwdriver
Wirecutters   Hammer
10 ml syringe   Hacksaw
Drill and bits   Woodglue

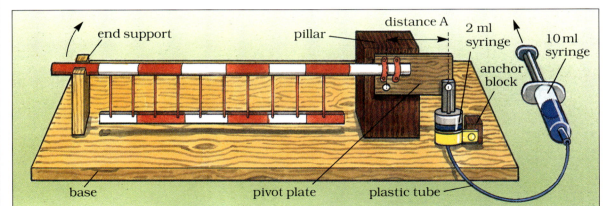

1. Glue and screw the pillar to the base, about 75 mm from one end. Drill small, evenly spaced holes in the alloy strip and barrier, as shown.

2. Drill the pivot plate for the pivot and syringe coupling. Fix the barrier to the pivot plate with the conduit clamps. Mount the pivot plate on the pillar. Trim the end support to length, so that the barrier rests level. Glue and screw the end support to the base.

3. Drill a hole, or cut a slot, in the syringe piston to fit the pivot. Assemble the syringe and fix it to the anchor block with the cable grip.

4. Glue and screw anchor block to the base. Cut and bend wire links for the barrier, to hold the bottom rail in position. Connect the syringes with the thin plastic tube and test the operation of the barrier. You may need to alter distance A – shorten it to make the gate open higher.

37

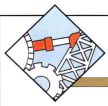

Robots

A robot testing car windscreens to check that they are tough enough.

Many of today's automatic machines are electronically controlled using microchips or computers. Some are machines that perform a single task, while others are more versatile. Their computers can be programmed and reprogrammed to enable them to perform a range of tasks. Their output is usually delivered by mechanical arms. These machines are known as robots.

The word 'robot' conjures up pictures of human-like devices, designed either as mechanical servants or as fearsome war machines. As yet, however, such machines are found only in science fiction stories. Real robots are rather different. They are factory machines, used for carrying out tasks that are repetitive, or involve working in unpleasant or dangerous conditions.

Such tasks include lifting, carrying, assembling parts, welding and painting.

The main features of a factory robot are the arm and the computer that controls it. A robot arm generally has six degrees of freedom, which means that it has six points at which different parts of the arm can move relative to each other. A 'waist' allows the arm to swivel, a 'shoulder' allows the whole arm to move up and down and an 'elbow' allows the forepart of the arm to be extended forwards and backwards. The remaining three degrees of freedom are provided by three joints in the wrist.

The arm can be equipped with a variety of different tools, such as grippers, drills, welding guns, glue guns, polishers and sprayers. What the robot does with the tool is controlled by the computer, which is often described as the robot's brain. This computer is programmed with a set of instructions and sends out signals to the motors that control the robot arm and tool. The instructions can be typed into the computer, using a keyboard and screen. Some robots can be 'trained' by a human controller, by being led through the movements needed to complete an operation. Spray-painting robots are trained in this way. The sequence of movements is recorded in the computer, which can then make the arm repeat the sequence again and again.

Like other automatic machines, robots use feedback to control their movements. Each joint of a robot arm has a position sensor that sends signals back to the computer. The latest robots are equipped with other sensors that enable them to grip objects gently and manipulate them very accurately. Scientists are working on ways of giving robots better senses and making them more intelligent.

Robots are used to assemble modern cars.

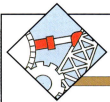

Build a robot arm

You need:
Wood base (250 mm x 250 mm x 12 mm thick)
Wood arm support (250 mm x 125 mm x 12 mm thick)
Wood jaw (50 mm x 20 mm x 12 mm thick)
Plastic tube (400 mm long: 18 mm diameter) for arm
Wood pivot block (30 mm x 30 mm x 12 mm thick)
6 x 10 ml syringes
1.5 m plastic tube to fit the syringes
6 x 15 mm pipe clips
3 conduit clamps
Alloy strip (20 mm x 2 mm x 250 mm)
Selection of nuts, bolts and screws
Hacksaw
Drill
File
Foam strip
Wax polish
Food colouring

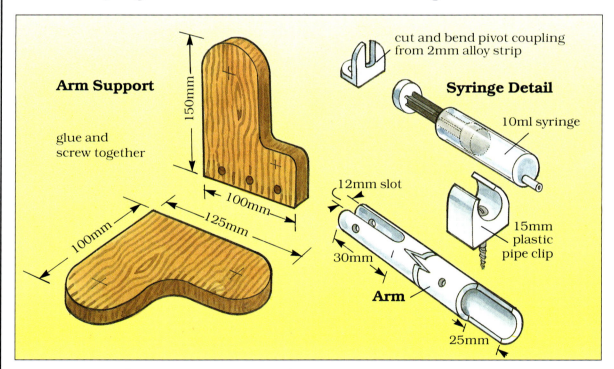

1. Cut out and shape the arm supports. Drill them for the pivot bolts. Glue and screw the two pieces together.

2. Drill holes in the arm tube, as shown. Drill, file and saw to cut the slots. Fasten the arm to the pivot block, about 75 mm from the end, using conduit clamps.

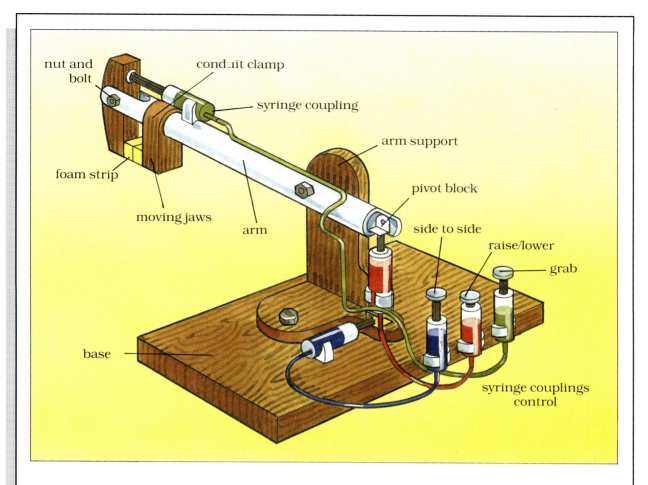

3. Cut out the moving jaws and drill holes to fit a nut and bolt. Slide the jaws into the arm slot. Fasten them with the nut and bolt. Attach the fixed arm with a conduit clamp and adjust until the jaws just pinch together. Attach the arm support to the base. Do not overtighten the nuts and bolts. All parts of the assembly should move freely without wobbling. A little wax polish will lubricate the joints.

4. Fix the syringe couplings as shown. Position the arm syringes. Allow plenty of plastic tube for free movement and attach to the control syringes, as shown.

5. Mix a drop of food colouring with water and prime each system by drawing water into the syringes. Make sure that all the air bubbles have been removed from the tubes. Clip the control syringes in place.

6. Move each syringe steadily to operate the arm smoothly. When you have mastered the controls, try moving a range of objects over obstacles and into containers. Paint the parts in bright colours.

7. Can you think of any other movements that you could build into your system? Can you make levers to operate the syringes?

Machines of the future

The earliest humans had no machines to help them. Over the centuries, a variety of machines have been invented and improved. Today, we rely on these machines for our survival. Without them, our modern way of life in the developed parts of the world would collapse.

We use machines for transport on land, on sea and in the air. We use machines to help us make things and we have devised machines to help us understand more about the world around us. Early machines were completely mechanical, but the discoveries and inventions concerned with electricity brought about a new generation of electromechanical machines.

Today, we still make use of mechanical and electromechanical machines. But, increasingly, electronic machines are playing an important part in our lives. For example, many of the machines used in medicine involve the use of electronic devices and computers. X-ray machines and brain scanners use complicated electronics, as do the patient-monitoring machines used in intensive care units. Some machines, such as heart-lung machines, kidney machines and other life-support machines, still rely on the use of electric motors, pumps and similar devices, but electronic machines are now vital to modern medicine.

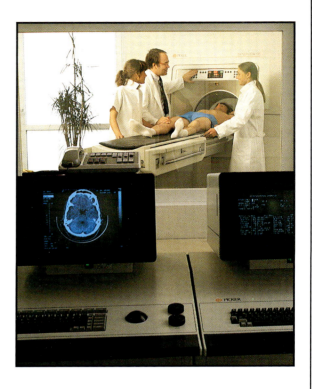

A CAT scanner uses X-rays and a computer to produce images of sections through a patient's brain.

Electronic devices are likely to play an increasing part in the machines of the future, whether they are used for transport, energy production, manufacture of goods or scientific research. However, it is not easy to predict the ways in which machine technology will develop in the future. There will undoubtedly be minor improvements made to existing types of machine. However, it is hard to imagine the development of major new types of machine that will be as important as, say, the

As yet, intelligent robots are found only in science fiction books and films. However, they may become commonplace in the future.

internal combustion engine, the aeroplane and television were during the early years of the twentieth century.

Many predictions come from science fiction. Writers predict that computers will become as intelligent as humans, and robots that behave exactly like humans will become part of everyday life. Scientists are now trying to devise intelligent computers, but there are many problems and the process is taking a long time. Science fiction writers would also have us believe that new technologies will be developed. Antigravity machines are predicted, as are spaceships that can travel through 'hyperspace' faster than the speed of light. But these will involve a complete change in the laws of physics as we understand them.

Glossary

Armature The rotating coil in an electric motor or generator.

Atmospheric pressure The weight of the layer of gases that surrounds the Earth.

Chemical energy The energy stored in the atoms or molecules of a substance.

Diaphragm A thin membrane or skin.

Diode An electronic device that allows electric current to pass in one direction only.

Electrical energy Energy in the form of an electric current.

Feedback A system in which the output of a machine is used to control the machine itself.

Field magnet One of the two stationary magnets in an electric motor or generator. The field magnets create the magnetic field in which the armature rotates.

Friction The force caused by two objects rubbing together.

Heat energy 1. Thermal energy contained in material as a result of the vibrating movement of its atoms or molecules. The greater the vibration, the hotter the material. 2. Radiated energy, of the same type as light, heat and radio waves. When radiant heat energy strikes an object, the object gains thermal energy and heats up. A hot object also gives out radiant heat energy.

Kinetic energy The energy contained in an object because it is moving. Thermal (heat) energy is a form of kinetic energy, due to the movement of atoms or molecules.

Mechanical advantage The ratio of a load to the force or effort needed to move it.

Micrometer A device for measuring thicknesses very accurately. A screw thread enables very small distances to be shown as much larger ones on a rotating scale.

Piston A cylindrical piece of material that fits tightly inside a hollow cylinder, but which can move to and fro.

Pivot A turning point.

Throttle A device in an internal combustion engine that controls the amount of fuel/air mixture reaching the cylinders.

Turbine A machine in which energy in a moving fluid, such as air or water, acts on two or more blades set on a shaft to produce rotating movement.

Valve A structure that controls the flow of a liquid, for example, or allows it to pass in one direction only.

Variable resistor A device in which the resistance to the flow of an electric current can be altered, thus altering the amount of current that flows.

Equipment

All the projects can be made with simple hand tools.
Junior hacksaws are good for cutting both wood and metal. Blades need to be sharp and secure in the frame with the teeth pointing forwards.
Panel-pin hammers are the easiest for small hands to use.
A wheel-brace hand drill and a selection of drill bits (2 mm to 9 mm) will make essential holes. Beware: small drills will cut through steel, but will break if not used with care!
A small file can be used to shape metal or plastic and will smooth wood.
Combination pliers are good for cutting, bending, twisting and holding.
Screws may be either slotted or crosshead, so a screwdriver to suit each sort is essential. Pick ones with comfortable handles that are not too large for the screws you will use.
Some form of work-holding device will make any project very much easier. G-clamps, a small clamp-on table vice or a work platform are good choices.
You may have to buy wood. Try to do this economically by setting out shapes on paper first, but remember that it is easier to make straight, rather than jigsaw-type, cuts. Check also to see if the grain direction of the timber is important. It might also be more efficient to stock up for two or three projects at once.
Dowel rod is used for axles and pivots. The most common size is 6 mm.
Metal may be more difficult to obtain. Most small engineering firms have a scrap box that will yield suitable light-weight sections, but be very careful of sharp edges.
Join metal pieces with nuts and bolts.
Join timber with screws, panel pins and woodworking glue. P.V.A. glue is excellent, but it must be squeezed tight with pins, screws or cramps and left overnight to dry.
For a smooth finish, use glass paper on wood and emery cloth on metal.
Apply colour to wood with colouring felts, or acrylic paints that enable brushes to be washed in water. Use an exterior-quality paint for metalwork or models that may be exposed to the weather.
All work should be carried out on a secure, steady surface. Protect it from paint etc. with newspaper.
Keep your tools sharp by storing them in a tool storage unit.

Notes for parents and teachers

This book will be useful to teachers in implementing the National Curriculum at Key Stages 1, 2 and 3. The information and activities relate to the following:

Technology attainment targets 1, 2, 3, 4 and 5.
Science attainment targets 1, 2, 3, 5, 6, 9, 10, 11, 12, 13, 14, 15 and 16.

Machines can also be developed as a cross-curricular topic that includes National Curriculum English and Mathematics.
   There are many activities in this book that will require the help of a teacher or parent.

Further information

Books to read

Catherall, E, *Exploring Uses of Energy* (Wayland, 1990)
Folsom, M and M, *The Macmillan Book of How Things Work* (Collier Macmillan, 1988)
Lambert, M, *Car Technology* (Wayland, 1989)
Macaulay, D, *The Way things Work* (Dorling Kindersley, 1989)
Rawson, C, *How Machines Work* (Usborne, 1988)
Exploring Technology series (Wayland)
Starting Technology series (Wayland)

Useful addresses

Australia

McEwans
(James McEwan & Co. Pty Ltd)
391 Bourke Street
North Ryde
New South Wales 2113

Pick Smith Electronics Pty Ltd
396 Lane Cove Road
Melbourne
Victoria 3000

Britain

Greater Manchester Museum of Science and Industry
Liverpool Road
Manchester

Science Museum
Exhibition Road
London SW7 2DD

Canada

N.C.R. Canada Ltd
320 Front Street West
Toronto
Ontario M5V 1B4

Philips Electronics Ltd
601 Milner Avenue
Scarborough
Ontario LAW 2T3

New Zealand

Mitre 10 NZ Ltd (D.I.Y.)
169 Wairau Road
Glenfield
Auckland 10

Phillips NZ Ltd (components)
110 Mt Eden Road
Mt Eden
Auckland

Index

Aeroplanes 14, 43
Antigravity 43
Archimedes 12
　screw pumps 31
Axles 8, 10, 14, 23

Bicycles 8
Binary code 34
Brakes 17

Cams 16
Cars 4, 17
Clocks 4, 10, 11
Compression stroke 22, 23
Computers 34, 38, 39, 42, 43
Crankshafts 23

Diesel engines 22

Effort 4, 6, 8
Electric circuits 16
　currents 24, 26, 32, 34, 36, 42
　motors 24, 25, 26, 32, 42
Electricity 14, 17, 24, 27, 42
Electronic machines 32, 34
Energy 4, 20, 26, 42
　chemical 4, 20
　electrical 4, 26
　heat 4, 20
　kinetic 4, 26
Engines 4, 17, 22, 23
Exhaust stroke 22
External combustion engines 22

Feedback 36, 41
Four-stroke cycle 22
Friction 8

Fuel 4, 17, 20, 22
Fulcrum 6, 8, 10

Gears 8, 10, 14, 34
Generators 26

Hydraulic systems 16, 17

Inclined planes 4, 12, 14, 32
Induction stroke 12
Internal combustion engines 17,
　22–3, 26, 43

Levers 4, 6, 8, 10, 14, 16, 23, 32,
　34
Loads 6, 8
Logic 34

Magnetism 24
Magnets 24
Mechanical advantage 6, 8
Microchips 40
Micrometers 13

Pendulums 10
Pistons 17, 22, 23, 30
Pivots 6, 7, 15
Pneumatic systems 17
Power 17
　stroke 22, 23
Pressure 17, 20, 22, 30, 36
Pulleys 8, 9
Pumps 14, 17, 30, 31, 32, 42

Robots 38–41, 43

Screws 12

Sensors 36, 39
Sorting 28–9, 35
Spark plugs 22
Steam 20, 21, 26
   engines 20
   turbines 20, 21
Switches 16, 17, 34, 38

Thyristor 17
Time 10
Tools 6, 12, 41

Valves 22, 30
Variable resistors 17

Wedges 4, 12
Wheels 4, 8, 10, 14, 16, 17, 23, 30, 32, 34
Winches 8
Windmills 14, 15
Work 4, 6, 20, 36

Picture acknowledgements

The photographs in this book were provided by: Eye Ubiquitous 36; Kobal 42; Mark Lambert 12, 17; TRH 23, 26, 34; Wayland Picture Library 28, 32; ZEFA *cover* 5, 14, 16, 18, 38, 39, 43. All artwork is by Stephen Wheele.